THE GAME OF

INFINITE

WEALTH & JOY

*The Link Between Effortless
Being and the Law of Attraction*

JOHN PEPPER

ROBERT RUGG

For inquiries, permissions, or speaking engagements:
robertrugg123@gmail.com

ISBN: 979-8-2874-9654-8
Published by Effortless Being Publications,
www.EffortlessBeing.net

Disclaimer: The experiences and insights shared in this book are the author's own and intended to provide information and inspiration for personal growth and self-realization. It is not a substitute for professional advice, and the author does not assume any responsibility for any results or consequences related to the application of the information in this book.

CONTENTS

Introduction

The Game You Were Born to Play

WHAT IF EVERYTHING YOU ever wanted—wealth, joy, freedom, and fulfillment—was already available to you? What if the secret to receiving it wasn't about effort, struggle, or even setting goals, but about allowing, playing, and aligning with who you truly are?

Welcome to *The Game of Infinite Wealth & Joy*.

This book isn't about working harder, hustling, or forcing reality to conform to your will. It's about discovering the effortless flow of existence—the place where life unfolds in your favor, abundance comes naturally, and you wake up every day feeling excited about the adventure ahead.

Why Call It a Game?

Because that's exactly what life is—a cosmic, infinite, ever-expanding playground. Somewhere along the way, many of us were conditioned to believe that life is hard, success requires struggle, and happiness must be earned. But when you look deeper, you'll find that none of those beliefs are actually true. They are rules of a game that someone else made up, and we've been playing along without questioning them.

Now, we invite you to play a new game. One where the rules are simple:

1. You are already infinitely abundant.

2. Life is meant to be joyful.

3. You attract what you are, not what you chase.

4. Wealth, love, and success come effortlessly when you align with your true self.

The moment you shift from striving to allowing, from effort to flow, you begin to experience the kind of wealth and joy that aren't dependent on external conditions—they arise from within, and they shape the world around you.

Effortless Being Meets the Law of Attraction

You may already be familiar with the Law of Attraction, which teaches that your thoughts create your reality. But there's a deeper dimension that isn't always emphasized—the space *before* thoughts, where infinite potential resides.

This space is what we call **Effortless Being**. It's not something you have to reach or attain—it's what you already are. When you shift into this awareness, manifestation stops being a struggle and becomes a natural side effect of your state of being.

In this book, we'll explore:

- ❖ How to stop chasing and start allowing.

- ❖ Why wealth and joy are already yours (and how to claim them).

- ❖ The truth about struggle—why it's optional.

- ❖ How to trust life so fully that abundance flows to you without effort.

- ❖ The key difference between force and flow.

A Journey We've Already Taken

This isn't just theory—it's lived experience.

We, Robert and John, didn't always live in effortless flow. Like many, we spent years trying to "figure it out," striving to manifest, and wondering why some things felt easy while others seemed impossible. Then, something shifted. We started to recognize the illusion of lack, the power of presence, and the effortless nature of true abundance. And once we saw it, we couldn't unsee it.

Now, we're here to share this understanding with you—not as teachers, but as guides who have walked this path and continue to play in this infinite game.

How to Use This Book

Each chapter is designed to shift your perception and open you up to a new way of being—one that feels light, fun, and deeply abundant. Read it cover to cover, or flip to the chapters that call to you. Most importantly, apply what resonates.

This book is not just something you read—it's something you live.

And if you're ready to step into a life where wealth and joy come effortlessly, then let's play.

Chapter 1

The Foundation of Infinite Wealth & Joy

Understanding Effortless Being & The Law of Attraction

The Game is Already Rigged in Your Favor

FROM THE MOMENT you were born, you were playing a game—one that most people don't even realize they're playing. It's called **The Game of Infinite Wealth and Joy**, and it's already designed for you to win. The problem? Most of us have been playing by someone else's rules, believing that life is hard, success requires struggle, and happiness is something we must earn.

But what if none of that is true? What if wealth and joy aren't things to chase, but things that arise naturally when we align with our true nature?

This is where **Effortless Being** and the **Law of Attraction** come together. They are two sides of the same coin. When you understand how they work together, manifestation becomes effortless, wealth flows, and joy is no longer something you seek—it's who you are.

What is Effortless Being?

Before we talk about how to attract wealth and joy, we need to understand who we truly are. At the deepest level, you are **not** your thoughts, your past, your struggles, or even the personality you believe yourself to be. You are **infinite being, pure consciousness, the effortless presence that has always been here**.

Effortless Being means:

❖ **You are not the doer.** Life unfolds effortlessly when you stop trying to control it.

❖ **You are already whole and complete.** There is nothing to fix, improve, or strive for—only to recognize.

❖ **Your natural state is joy, abundance, and freedom.** Anything that feels like lack, struggle, or effort is coming from the mind's conditioning, not from reality itself.

When you relax into your true nature, you **stop chasing and start allowing**. Manifestation stops feeling like a technique and becomes a natural byproduct of your state of being.

The Law of Attraction: A Deeper Perspective

You've probably heard of the Law of Attraction before—it's the idea that "like attracts like." Whatever energy you put out, you attract back into your experience. If you focus on abundance, you attract more abundance. If you focus on lack, you attract more lack.

Sounds simple, right? Then why doesn't it always work?

Because most people focus on **what they lack while pretending to be abundant.** They visualize wealth while *feeling* broke. They say affirmations about joy while *feeling* anxious.

The Law of Attraction doesn't respond to your words or even your thoughts—it responds to **your state of being.**

That's why *Effortless Being* is the missing key. When you embody abundance as your natural state—not through effort, but through recognition—life has no choice but to reflect that back to you.

How Effortless Being and the Law of Attraction Work Together

Most manifestation teachings start at the level of the mind: think positive, visualize, affirm. But that approach still assumes **you** are the one making things happen.

Effortless Being, on the other hand, takes you deeper. It shows you that manifestation isn't something you do—it's something that **happens naturally when you align with your true nature**.

Here's how it works:

1. **You recognize you are already whole, complete, and infinitely abundant.** There is no lack—only the illusion of lack.

2. **You relax into this knowing.** You don't try to manifest; you simply recognize that everything is already unfolding for you.

3. **You allow life to move effortlessly through you.** Without resistance, everything begins to flow in unexpected and effortless ways.

The Law of Attraction is no longer something you "use." It becomes **a natural expression of who you are**.

The Illusion of Hard Work and Effort

One of the biggest myths we've been conditioned to believe is that success and wealth require hard work. But if that were true, wouldn't the hardest-working people be the wealthiest?

Instead, the wealthiest people often work *less*—not because they're lazy, but because they operate from **alignment, not effort**. They don't chase success; they allow it. They don't grind their way to wealth; they align with abundance and let it flow.

This doesn't mean you never take action. But action from **alignment** feels completely different than action from **struggle**. Aligned action is inspired, joyful, and effortless. Struggle is exhausting, forced, and filled with doubt.

Shifting from Struggle to Flow

To begin playing the game the right way, you must let go of the belief that effort equals results. Instead, shift into **effortless alignment** by:

1. **Letting go of the need to "make things happen."** Trust that everything you need is already coming to you.

2. **Following what feels expansive and exciting.** Your excitement is a compass pointing you toward alignment.

3. **Recognizing that life is happening for you, not to you.** Everything in your experience is perfectly designed to awaken you to your true nature.

The more you relax, the more you will see that wealth and joy are not things you create—they are **states of being** that naturally attract everything you desire.

Playing the Game

Now that you understand the foundation of infinite wealth and joy, it's time to start playing.

Here's the rule: **Stop trying. Start being.**

The moment you stop trying to be wealthy, joyful, or successful, and simply recognize that you already are—everything shifts. Wealth flows, joy expands, and life begins to feel like the game it was always meant to be.

Chapter 2

The Illusion of Lack – Shifting from Scarcity to Abundance Effortlessly

Lack is an Illusion—But It Feels So Real

IMAGINE A FISH SWIMMING in the ocean, constantly searching for water. It's swimming *in* water, surrounded *by* water, yet it's convinced that it needs to find water to survive.

This is how most of us live when it comes to abundance. We are already immersed in it, yet we've been conditioned to believe that we must *struggle* to attain it. We say things like:

- ➤ "I don't have enough money."
- ➤ "I need to work harder to be successful."
- ➤ "I want more freedom, but I feel trapped."

But here's the thing—**lack does not actually exist.** It's a mental concept, a belief system we inherited from society, family, and past experiences. In reality, **life is infinitely abundant, and everything you need is already flowing to you effortlessly.** The only reason it *feels* like lack exists is because we've been taught to focus on what's missing rather than on what's already here.

So, how do we break free from the illusion of lack? The first step is to recognize how deeply embedded this belief is—and then to see through it.

The Mind's Game of Scarcity

Your mind operates like a filter. It doesn't show you *reality*—it shows you what you **believe** to be true.

If you believe money is scarce, your mind will show you evidence of financial struggle everywhere. If you believe opportunities are limited, you'll only see doors closing. But the moment you shift your belief, reality shifts with you.

This is why two people can experience the same event in completely different ways. One person might lose their job and see it as a crisis, feeling trapped in scarcity. Another might lose their job and feel excited, seeing it as an opportunity for something greater.

Same event, two completely different experiences.

The difference? **Their inner state.**

The truth is, **you are creating your reality in every moment by what you focus on.** When you shift your focus from lack to abundance, the entire game changes.

Effortless Being and the End of Lack

Here's where **Effortless Being** comes in. The reason lack feels so real is because we are still identifying with the *character* in the game, the one who believes they have to struggle to win. But when we step back and recognize that we are the **infinite being behind it all**, lack dissolves instantly.

In your direct experience, right now—are you lacking anything?

Look around. Right here, right now, are you actually missing something? Or is lack just a thought in your mind, a belief system that you've been conditioned into?

When you realize that you **are already whole, already abundant**, the game of chasing and striving stops. You no longer feel the need to work harder, struggle more, or fight for what you want. Instead, you relax into **allowing**—and from this state, abundance flows effortlessly.

The Law of Attraction and Your Set Point of Abundance

The Law of Attraction is always working—it doesn't turn on and off. The question is: **What frequency are you broadcasting?**

Most people unknowingly broadcast lack. They say they want abundance, but they feel scarcity. And the Universe doesn't respond to what you *say* you want—it responds to your **state of being**.

If you feel abundant, you attract abundance.

If you feel joy, you attract more experiences that amplify that joy.

If you feel struggle, you attract more struggle.

So, the key isn't to try harder to manifest abundance—it's to shift into the **feeling** of already being abundant.

How to Shift from Lack to Abundance Effortlessly

So how do we shift our default setting from scarcity to abundance? Here are a few effortless shifts that dissolve lack instantly:

1. Stop "Wanting" and Start Recognizing What's Already Here

Wanting something creates a sense of separation—it tells the Universe, "I don't have this yet." But abundance isn't something to acquire—it's something to recognize.

Instead of saying, "I want more money," try shifting to:

❖ "I love how abundance is always flowing to me in unexpected ways."

❖ "I appreciate the wealth that already exists in my life."

❖ "Money and opportunities find me effortlessly."

Notice how these statements aren't trying to make something happen. They are simply acknowledging what's already true.

2. Play the "Already Abundant" Game

Imagine you wake up tomorrow, and you know without a doubt that you are infinitely abundant. How would you walk, talk, and act differently?

❖ Would you check your bank account in fear, or would you trust that money is always coming?

❖ Would you feel anxious about bills, or would you feel excitement about the flow of wealth in your life?

JOHN PEPPER & ROBERT RUGG

When you start embodying the energy of abundance NOW, reality has no choice but to mirror it back to you.

3. Let Go of "How" and Focus on "Yes"

One of the biggest ways we block abundance is by obsessing over how it's going to come. But the "how" is not your job—that's the Universe's job.

Your only job is to stay open to the yes.

Start saying yes to abundance in all forms:

➢ Receive compliments without deflecting them.

➢ Accept help when it's offered.

➢ Appreciate the money you already have, no matter how small.

The more you say yes, the more the Universe will bring you things to say yes to.

4. Shift from "Not Enough" to "More Than Enough"

Abundance is a state of mind. The moment you decide you already have more than enough, your reality shifts.

Try this:

❖ Instead of thinking, "I need more time," shift to: "I have all the time I need."

❖ Instead of "I need more money," shift to: "I love the wealth that's already in my life."

❖ Instead of "I wish I had more freedom," shift to: "I already feel free in so many ways."

The more you recognize what's already here, the more of it you'll attract.

The Game of Abundance is Effortless

You don't have to fight for abundance. It's your natural state. The only thing that ever blocked it was the belief in lack—and now you see that lack is just a mental illusion.

The Game of Infinite Wealth & Joy isn't about getting more. It's about realizing that you already are more than enough.

And the best part?

When you shift your state of being, life responds. Wealth flows. Opportunities appear. Joy expands. All without effort.

Because when you recognize the game, you stop struggling—and start playing.

Chapter 3

Aligning with the Flow – How to Stay in the Energy of Receiving Effortlessly

Abundance is Already Flowing—Are You Letting It In?

IMAGINE A RIVER constantly flowing with ease, moving effortlessly around rocks, bends, and obstacles. The river doesn't push, strain, or force its way—it simply flows.

This is how abundance naturally works. It is always flowing toward you, ready to pour into your life in infinite ways.

The only question is: Are you allowing it, or are you resisting it?

Most people unknowingly block their own abundance by getting stuck in patterns of doubt, effort, and control. They think, "I need to figure this out" or "I need to make this happen." But in reality, the more you try to force something, the more you block it.

True abundance doesn't require effort—it requires alignment. And when you're aligned, receiving becomes effortless.

The Key to Receiving: Stop Holding the Door Shut

Think of a door that naturally swings open. If you do nothing, it stays open effortlessly. But the moment you try to force it open, you're actually pushing against it.

This is exactly what happens when we try too hard to manifest something. Our very effort contradicts the state of already having it.

Effort says: "I don't have this yet."

Alignment says: "It's already mine."

Your abundance is already here—the only thing that ever delayed it was the resistance created by effort and doubt.

Step 1: Shift from Doing to Allowing

Most people approach abundance with a doing mindset.

"I need to make more money."

"I need to figure out my purpose."

"I need to manifest the perfect relationship."

But abundance isn't something you have to chase—it's something you allow.

When you are in the energy of allowing, things come to you effortlessly.

You've probably noticed this before:

➤ The moment you stop obsessing over something, it finally happens.

➤ When you take a break from work, creative ideas suddenly flow in.

➤ When you stop worrying about money, unexpected income shows up.

This is because the need to do creates resistance, while the energy of allowing creates flow.

Try this shift:

❖ Instead of saying, "What do I need to do to make this happen?", shift to "How can I open up and let this in?"

❖ Instead of focusing on what's missing, shift to appreciating what's already flowing.

Abundance flows to those who are open to receiving. The key is not effort—but alignment.

Step 2: Get into the Receiving State (It's Already Done)

The secret to receiving isn't about asking for more—it's about aligning with what's already yours.

Right now, the version of you that has everything you want already exists. Your only job is to shift into that frequency and become the person who naturally receives it.

How to Do This Effortlessly:

* ❖ Imagine it's already done – Instead of wanting something, practice the feeling of already having it. How does it feel to know it's inevitable?

* ❖ Focus on the joy of having, not the lack of wanting – Feel the excitement of abundance already being yours.

* ❖ Relax into trust – When you know something is yours, you stop stressing about it. Adopt the mindset: "It's already on its way."

Step 3: Master the Art of Non-Interference

One of the biggest ways people block their own receiving is by interfering with the process.

Have you ever planted a seed and then dug it up every day to check if it's growing? Of course not! You plant it, water it, and trust that it will grow.

But when it comes to abundance, many people do the opposite. They:

- ✓ Obsess over when their manifestation will arrive.

- ✓ Worry about how it's going to happen.

- ✓ Keep "checking" reality to see if it's working.

This constant interference slows the process down.

The truth is, the universe is already working on your behalf. Your only job is to get out of the way and let it happen.

How to Stop Interfering:

- ❖ Let go of the "when" and "how" – The more you micromanage, the more resistance you create.

- ❖ Trust that the universe has perfect timing – It's unfolding in ways better than you could plan.

- ❖ Practice detachment – When you stop needing something to happen, it happens faster.

Step 4: Follow the Path of Least Resistance

Have you ever noticed that when you force something, it rarely works—but when you relax, everything falls into place?

This is because abundance follows the path of least resistance.

You don't need to push against obstacles—you simply need to align with what already wants to flow to you.

Imagine being in a lazy river, floating effortlessly. You can try to swim upstream, or you can let go and flow effortlessly in the direction life is already carrying you.

How to Align with the Flow:

➤ Follow what feels light and easy – The universe speaks through ease, not struggle.

➤ Trust your excitement – If something excites you, it's a sign you're on the right path.

➤ Stop forcing what isn't working – Resistance is a sign to let go and flow in a different direction.

Step 5: Say Yes to the Signs of Abundance

Most people don't recognize how much abundance is already flowing to them. They think they are "waiting" for wealth, love, or success—when in reality, it's already showing up in small ways.

The universe always gives you breadcrumbs before it gives you the full manifestation.

For example:

❖ A random check arrives in the mail.

❖ A stranger offers you help unexpectedly.

❖ An opportunity comes out of nowhere.

These are signs that abundance is already in motion!

How to Open the Floodgates of Receiving:

➤ Celebrate every small sign of abundance – Treat every gift, opportunity, and synchronicity as proof that the universe is working for you.

➤ Say yes more often – Be open to receiving in all forms, even the unexpected ones.

➤ Appreciate what's already flowing – Gratitude amplifies the flow of wealth, joy, and opportunities.

Abundance is Effortless—The Only Question is, Are You Open to It?

You don't need to work harder to receive. You don't need to struggle to be worthy.

Abundance is already here. Your only job is to align, allow, and say yes.

Recap of the Receiving Formula:

❖ Stop trying to force abundance—align with it instead.

❖ Shift from doing to allowing.

❖ Get into the state of already having.

❖ Stop interfering—let the universe work for you.

❖ Follow the path of least resistance.

❖   Say yes to every sign of abundance.

When you align with these principles, life becomes effortless. Abundance finds you. Wealth flows in unexpected ways. Joy becomes your natural state.

Because in the *Game of Infinite Wealth & Joy*, the winners aren't the ones who try the hardest.

The winners are the ones who allow the most.

Chapter 4

The Art of Playing the Game – Life as a Joyful, Effortless Experiment

Life is a Game—Are You Playing or Struggling?

MOST PEOPLE TAKE LIFE way too seriously. They treat their goals as heavy burdens, their challenges as battles to be won, and their daily experience as something to "get through." But what if life wasn't meant to be so serious? What if life was a game—a grand experiment where the goal is not to struggle, but to play?

When we approach life as an experiment rather than a test, everything changes. Instead of fearing failure, we become curious. Instead of resisting change, we embrace it. And instead of feeling pressured to control every outcome, we learn to trust the process.

Effortless abundance is not about forcing success. It's about playing the game with joy, curiosity, and lightness.

Releasing the Need for Control

One of the biggest reasons people struggle in life is that they're trying to control outcomes. They set rigid expectations, attach to specific results, and resist anything that doesn't go according to plan. But the truth is, the more you try to control life, the harder it becomes.

Imagine trying to control every single wave in the ocean—you'd exhaust yourself! But if you learn to surf the waves instead of resisting them, suddenly, the ocean becomes your ally, not your enemy.

That's what playing the game of life is about—riding the waves instead of fighting them.

Non-Attachment: The Key to Winning the Game Effortlessly

The secret to effortless abundance is non-attachment. This doesn't mean you stop wanting things—it means you stop needing them.

When you let go of attachment:

➢ You still set intentions, but you're not desperate for a specific outcome.

➤ You take inspired action, but you don't force things to happen.

➤ You allow life to unfold, knowing that the best possible path is already being revealed.

When you detach, you stop clenching, striving, and chasing. Instead, you trust, relax, and receive. Life begins to unfold effortlessly because you're no longer in resistance.

Turning Life Into a Playground

Children are the ultimate masters of effortless being. They don't wake up stressing about their purpose, financial security, or success. They simply follow what feels fun, exciting, and natural—and in doing so, they learn, grow, and create with ease.

This is the essence of effortless manifestation. When you treat life as a playground:

❖ You experiment without fear of failure.

❖ You take action from excitement, not pressure.

❖ You trust that the right opportunities will arise effortlessly.

Play doesn't mean passivity. It means active, engaged, and joyful participation in life without attachment to the outcome.

The irony is, the less seriously you take the game, the more success flows to you naturally.

Playing with the Energy of Life

If life is a game, then energy is the currency. Every moment, you are playing with energy—your thoughts, emotions, and focus shape your experience.

Ask yourself:

➢ Am I playing this game from stress, fear, or doubt?

➢ Or am I playing with lightness, trust, and ease?

Energy flows where attention goes. The more you focus on expansion, joy, and curiosity, the more life reflects those experiences back to you.

Real-Life Reflections: A Shift From Pressure to Play

Before: John used to live like life was a giant to-do list. He was constantly planning, pushing, and performing—even in his spiritual practice. Every meditation, affirmation, or technique was part of a strategy to "get somewhere."

He wasn't playing the game... he was trying to control it.

Turning Point: Things began to shift when John heard one simple question: *"What if this gets to be fun?"*

Something clicked.

He started letting go of pressure and following what felt natural. He didn't stop taking action—he just stopped trying to force outcomes. He let joy lead the way.

After: John began treating life like a grand experiment. He:

- ➢ Said yes to what felt light, and no to what felt heavy.
- ➢ Followed intuitive nudges instead of mental calculations.
- ➢ Focused on how he felt—not what he thought he needed.

And the results? Effortless.

Countless job offers started coming to him out of nowhere. Abundance showed up in unexpected ways. Even his health improved—not from trying harder, but from relaxing more deeply.

Key Realization: *"I realized I was the one creating the pressure. When I dropped the script and just played, life met me with flow. Everything I thought I needed to force... began showing up naturally."*

How to Experiment with Life Today

If you want to start playing life as a game instead of struggling through it, try these experiments:

> ➤ **Play with "What If?"**

Instead of worrying about failure, play the game of *"What if this works out better than I imagined?"*

Try it for a day—see what happens when you assume everything is working in your favor.

> ➤ **Follow the Path of Least Resistance**

If something feels forced, step back and ask, *"What would feel lighter and more natural right now?"*

Move toward the path that feels effortless and exciting.

> ➤ **Detach from Specific Outcomes for a Week**

Set an intention, but don't micromanage how it happens.

Observe how life brings unexpected solutions when you let go.

> ➤ **Say Yes to Play**

Do something purely for fun—without any expectation of productivity or results.

Notice how play opens up creativity and flow in unexpected ways.

Winning the Game Effortlessly

The only way to lose in life is to forget that it's a game. If you're struggling, stressing, or pushing too hard, step back and remember:

Life is a playground. Abundance is a game. Effortlessness is the key.

Play the game with trust, ease, and joy—and watch how the universe plays back.

Chapter 5

Beyond Effort – The Secret to Manifesting Effortlessly

The Myth of Hard Work:
Why 'Trying Hard' Blocks Wealth and Joy

FOR MOST OF OUR LIVES, we've been conditioned to believe that effort equals results.

"No pain, no gain."

"Work hard, and you'll succeed."

"If you're not struggling, you're not trying hard enough."

But what if this is completely backward?

Look at the wealthiest, happiest, and most fulfilled people. Are they grinding 24/7, sacrificing joy, and forcing success? No. The most abundant people are those who have mastered effortless alignment. They are in a state of flow where everything they need shows up at the perfect time—not because they forced it, but because they aligned with it.

The truth is: Wealth, joy, and success are not things to chase. They are states of being you align with.

If success was about effort, the hardest workers would be the richest. But we all know people who hustle endlessly and never seem to get ahead. Why? Because they are playing the wrong game—the game of force instead of flow.

How Effort Creates Resistance
Have you ever noticed that the more you try to make something happen, the more resistance you encounter?

- ❖ You stress about money → unexpected bills keep showing up.

- ❖ You desperately want love → relationships feel out of reach.

- ❖ You force an idea to work → everything feels blocked and frustrating.

Why does this happen? Because forcing something signals lack.

Effort is rooted in the belief that what you want is not already here. It's a vibration of scarcity, struggle, and doubt. The more you push, the more the universe mirrors back that struggle.

The Secret: Letting Things Come to You

So, what's the alternative? Receiving effortlessly.

Manifestation isn't about effort—it's about alignment.

Imagine two people planting a tree:

➢ Person A digs aggressively, shovels water in, and demands the tree grow faster.

➢ Person B plants it with care, waters it, and trusts nature's timing.

Who do you think will see better results?

Effortless manifestation is like planting seeds and allowing them to grow. You don't dig up your seeds every day to check if they're sprouting—you trust the process.

How to Shift from Forcing to Flowing

1. Recognize the Illusion of Effort

➢ The universe is already set up to bring you what you need.

➢ Struggle is a sign you're trying too hard instead of aligning.

➢ The moment you drop effort, life begins to flow.

2. **Move from Desperation to Expectation**

> Desperation says: "I need this to happen or else."

> Expectation says: "Of course, this is coming to me."

> Start expecting good things with relaxed confidence.

3. **Act from Inspiration, Not Obligation**

> Forced action comes from fear, lack, and needing control.

> Inspired action feels light, effortless, and exciting.

> Ask yourself: "Does this feel like flow, or does this feel like force?"

Effortless Manifestation in Action

Let's look at two different ways to manifest wealth:

The Effort-Based Way:

❖ Wake up stressed about money

❖ Force yourself to work extra hours

❖ Overthink and worry about bills

❖ Hustle, grind, and sacrifice

❖ Still feel like it's not enough

The Effortless Way:

❖ Relax into the knowing that abundance is already flowing

❖ Follow your excitement and trust inspired action

❖ Release attachment to how money shows up

❖ Enjoy your life, knowing wealth is inevitable

❖ Unexpected opportunities and money appear effortlessly

Which reality feels lighter?

Which version would you rather live?

The Law of Least Effort

Nature operates effortlessly. A tree doesn't struggle to grow. A river doesn't force its way—it follows the path of least resistance.

When you align with the natural flow of life, things come to you without strain.

The Law of Least Effort states:

➢ The easier it feels, the more aligned you are.

➢ If it feels forced, it's not your path.

➢ When you stop resisting, what you want flows effortlessly.

Have you ever stopped looking for something, and the moment you let go, it appears?

That's the Law of Least Effort in action.

Trusting Life to Do the Heavy Lifting

Most of us think we are the ones making things happen. But in reality, life is unfolding effortlessly.

- ❖ Your heart beats without effort.

- ❖ The sun rises without effort.

- ❖ Your breath flows naturally.

Manifestation works the same way. The less you force it, the more effortlessly it unfolds.

How to Start Manifesting Without Effort

1. **Relax Your Grip on Reality**

   ➢ Stop overthinking, stop forcing, stop controlling.

   ➢ Life knows what it's doing—let it unfold naturally.

2. **Follow What Feels Light and Fun**

   ➢ Struggle is not required to be successful.

   ➢ If something feels heavy, drop it. If it feels exciting, do more of it.

3. Trust in the Timing

> ➢ The right people, opportunities, and wealth are already aligning for you.

> ➢ If something hasn't shown up yet, it's because it's still on its way.

Playing the Manifestation Game

To fully embrace effortless manifestation, try this experiment:

For 7 days, commit to this:

- ❖ Take no action from fear or desperation.
- ❖ Only follow what excites you.
- ❖ Trust that what you want is already done.
- ❖ If it feels hard, let it go.

At the end of the week, notice:

- ❖ Did life feel lighter?
- ❖ Did unexpected things flow effortlessly?
- ❖ Did you experience more ease, abundance, and joy?

This is how manifestation was meant to work.

Real-Life Reflections: Effortless Manifestation

What was the biggest shift that helped you realize alignment is more powerful than effort?

Literally today, I felt an excited impulse to go to a coffee shop and allow some words of this book to flow through me. I ordered a drink that is, by default, prepared with ice, but specifically asked for no ice. When they called my name, I picked up my coffee and looked at it—sure enough, ice was in the drink, even though the order sticker said "no ice."

I paused and chose my thoughts: Everyone's doing their best. I've missed instructions before. This coffee is delicious either way. There's nothing to resist. This was a small, fun, conscious opportunity to let go and be in Effortless Being.

I smiled, took the drink, sat down, and opened my laptop. Just then, a barista walked over, smiling, "Hey, I realized I made yours with ice—I'll remake it with no ice. Keep the other one if you want."

Goosebumps. I received twice what I ordered and did nothing to make it happen. This wasn't about the coffee. It was a vivid demonstration of what happens when we're in a state of Effortless Being.

And yes, I had the thought, "It's just a coffee." But then I realized—that thought is exactly what illuminated the deeper truth: I was labeling things as big or small. And that is the resistance.

When we remove the labels of "big deal" and "small deal," life flows. Nothing is a big deal. Nothing is a small deal. Nothing is a deal.

Can You Share an Example?

Can you share an example where you trusted the flow instead of forcing, and it paid off beyond what you imagined?

Years ago, I was excited to buy my first condo. My finances and energy were aligned. The very first place I saw felt perfect. I made an offer. It was accepted. We were under contract. It felt effortless.

Then, the inspection came. Significant water damage. Ongoing lawsuits. A major red flag.

Instead of forcing it, I leaned back and trusted. I remembered—I already had a great place to live. This was an experiment in abundance, not a necessity.

A few days later, my realtor found a new listing. Same neighborhood. A building I had admired countless times but assumed was out of reach.

It wasn't.

Not only was it in my price range, but the unit was filled with deeply meaningful details:

- ➢ The same lighting design as my grandfather's house.

- ➢ A pebble rock shower floor matching a beloved bath mat I'd owned for a decade.

- ➢ Drinking glasses identical to ones I had cherished since childhood.

Now, I live there. Every day I say: Look at where I live!

It was all so effortless. So perfectly aligned.

Effortless. Law of Attraction. It's just how it is.

Effortless Abundance: The New Paradigm

The old paradigm says:

- ❖ You must struggle for success.

- ❖ Hard work is the only way to get ahead.

- ❖ If you don't hustle, you'll fall behind.

The new paradigm says:

- ❖ Alignment creates more wealth than effort.

- ❖ Life supports you when you trust it.

- ❖ The less you chase, the more flows to you.

When you surrender the need to "make things happen" and step into effortless allowing, wealth and joy no longer feel like a goal—they become your natural state.

Final Thought: Let It Be Easy

If you take away one lesson from this chapter, let it be this:

Let it be easy.

Life is not supposed to be a struggle.

Abundance is not something you fight for—it is something you allow.

The moment you decide that ease is the new normal, the universe responds.

Your only job? Trust, relax, and let it flow.

Chapter 6

Tuning into Your Infinite Nature – How to Access Your Highest Self in Daily Life

The Key to Effortless Abundance: Recognizing Yourself as the Source

IMAGINE FOR A MOMENT that everything you desire—wealth, love, clarity, purpose—already exists within you. What if abundance wasn't something you needed to get, but something you needed to remember?

Your highest self—your infinite nature—is already whole, complete, and effortlessly abundant. It is always present, waiting for you to shift into awareness. The only thing that ever blocks you from this truth is identification with the limited self—the part of you that believes it must strive, chase, and control in order to succeed.

But here's the truth: You are the source of everything you seek.

The moment you stop looking outward for fulfillment and start aligning with your infinite nature, life begins to unfold effortlessly. The struggle dissolves. Manifestation becomes second nature. Joy, clarity, and abundance become your default state.

The Difference Between the Limited Self and the Infinite Being

Most people live from a limited identity, which is why they experience struggle. This identity is built on thoughts, beliefs, and conditioning that reinforce a sense of separation.

Limited Self (Ego Mode)

➤ Feels disconnected from abundance.

➤ Operates from fear, doubt, and effort.

➤ Tries to control outcomes.

➤ Seeks happiness in external achievements.

➤ Reacts to circumstances instead of creating from alignment.

Infinite Self (Effortless Being Mode)

➤ Knows abundance is always flowing.

➤ Trusts life and follows ease.

➤ Aligns with inspiration rather than force.

➤ Recognizes happiness as an internal state.

➤ Responds with wisdom rather than reacting with fear.

Shifting into your infinite nature doesn't mean becoming something new—it means remembering what you already are. It's about unlearning the false identity and relaxing into the effortless intelligence that has always been here.

How to Tap into Your Infinite Nature Effortlessly

1. Shift Your Perspective: You Are Not Your Thoughts

➤ Notice your thoughts, but don't believe them.

➤ See thoughts as passing clouds—not reality itself.

➤ Ask yourself: Who is observing these thoughts?

That silent awareness behind the thoughts? That's you. That's your infinite nature. The more you rest in this awareness, the more effortlessly life flows.

2. The Practice of Presence: Living in the Now

Your infinite self exists only in the present moment. Struggle, worry, and lack arise when your mind is focused on the past or the future.

➤ Worrying about money? That's a future problem.

- ➢ Regretting a decision? That's a past loop.

- ➢ But right now, in this moment? Everything is okay.

Try this:

- ❖ Pause. Breathe deeply.

- ❖ Notice your surroundings—colors, sounds, sensations.

- ❖ Ask: Is there any lack right now?

- ❖ Feel the peace of presence.

That peace? That's your true self.

3. Recognizing Your Infinite Intelligence

Effortless being is not passive—it is intelligently active. The more you align with your infinite nature, the more you realize you already know what to do.

- ➢ Inspired ideas flow.

- ➢ Synchronicities align.

- ➢ Opportunities unfold.

Ask yourself:

- ❖ What feels expansive right now?

- ❖ What action feels light and effortless?

- ❖ What naturally excites me in this moment?

These subtle nudges are your highest self guiding you.

The Power of Surrender: Trusting Life to Support You

The limited self believes it must control everything. But your infinite self knows life is always supporting you.

The secret to effortless manifestation is surrendering control.

When you stop gripping so tightly, life moves for you:

- ❖ The right people appear.

- ❖ Money flows in unexpected ways.

- ❖ Opportunities align perfectly.

You're not blocking the flow—you're allowing it.

Trusting the Flow: A Real-Life Example

Think about a time something happened effortlessly—an unexpected check, a chance encounter, or perfect timing.

Did you force it?

Or did it show up when you were relaxed, present, and trusting?

That's alignment. That's effortless being.

How to Stay in Your Infinite Nature Daily

Morning Alignment Practice

- Begin your day with stillness.

- Sit for 5 minutes and feel the peace that's already here.

Follow What Feels Light

- Your excitement is your compass.

- If it feels like force, pause. If it feels light, lean in.

Trust the First Thought

- The first inspired idea is usually the one.

- Don't overthink it—just follow the flow.

Say Yes to Flow, No to Force

- Struggle = stop.

- Shift to allowing.

- Trust the abundance is on its way.

Real-Life Reflections: Daily Practices for Effortless Alignment

The absolute coolest "manifestation" I can imagine at this point in my life is consciously, experientially, and viscerally knowing—with complete and utter certainty—that I am the creator of my own reality, that I can be, do, and have anything, and above all else, that I know how to engage my own creation mechanism.

That's why first thing every day, I intentionally and excitedly set aside time to remind myself that my inner thoughts, emotions, and feelings are the highest priority. These inner processes are the upstream creation point for my "outer" experience.

I have a whole toolbox of feel-good practices I pull from intuitively—meditation, imagination breaks, beautiful social media content, going to joyful events, and re-listening to the truth of Effortless Being and The Law of Attraction.

And of course, I love tuning into my favorite source:

The Game of Infinite Wealth & Joy by Robert Rugg & John Pepper.

Can You Share a Moment When Trusting Your Higher Self Over Logic Created an Unexpected Windfall?

About a year ago, I was super into trading stocks. One day, after a blissful meditation, I felt an impulse to buy a certain stock—even though I knew nothing about it.

I followed that impulse with zero logic.

Minutes into market open, the stock exploded in value. I sold. Then the stock dropped. I bought again. It surged again. I repeated this almost twenty times during the day, laughing with joy.

I literally felt like the market was saying:

"You like that? Here's more. Here's more. Here's more."

It was my most fun, profitable, and intuitive trading day ever.

But more than the money, I saw the deeper abundance: the fun, the trust, the thrill of co-creating with life itself. It was the perfect example of how probabilities are always 100% at the intersection of Effortless Being and the Law of Attraction.

Effortless Success Comes from Living as Your Infinite Self

Most people chase success from the limited self—and suffer. When you remember your true nature, success, wealth, and joy come to you.

Biggest takeaway?

You are already the abundance you seek.

The more you live from this truth, the easier life becomes.

Chapter 7

Vibrational Wealth – Raising Your Frequency for Effortless Abundance

The Frequency of Wealth and Joy

EVERYTHING IN THE UNIVERSE is vibration—including you.

Money, love, joy, clarity, creativity—they all exist as energetic frequencies. When you tune into the frequency of wealth, you become a match for it. You don't chase abundance—you resonate with it.

You've probably experienced this before: when you're feeling good, confident, and at ease, things flow to you effortlessly. People compliment you. Opportunities show up. Your day unfolds with synchronicity. That's not an accident. That's alignment.

The more you raise your frequency to match wealth, joy, and expansion, the more naturally those experiences flow into your life.

The truth is: you don't attract what you want—you attract what you are.

So ask yourself: Am I being a vibrational match to the life I want? Or am I operating from the vibration of lack, doubt, and worry?

Shifting your vibration is not about pretending to be happy—it's about tapping into the part of you that is already whole, already abundant, already free.

Aligning with Your Natural State

Your natural state is joy. Peace. Presence. Aliveness.

But for most people, that state gets covered up with mental clutter: overthinking, limiting beliefs, unprocessed emotions, and stories of not-enoughness.

When you release those layers, you don't have to "raise" your vibration—it rises on its own. Here are a few simple shifts that align you with your natural, high-vibe state:

Gratitude for What Is

Gratitude isn't just a feel-good practice—it's an instant frequency boost. When you focus on what you appreciate right now, you're no longer resisting what is. You are aligning with the energy of enoughness, which is magnetic to more.

Ask:

> ➢ What feels good in my life right now?

> ➢ What small thing can I appreciate in this moment?

Follow What Feels Expansive

The fastest way to raise your vibration is to follow your excitement. When something feels light, expansive, or joyful—it's your inner being guiding you.

Small joys matter: a song you love, a funny video, a spontaneous dance in your kitchen. The more often you follow these impulses, the more your life becomes a magnet for miracles.

Drop the Thoughts That Don't Serve You

Not every thought deserves your attention. Some are simply echoes of old conditioning.

Ask:

➢ Does this thought expand me or contract me?

➢ Would my highest self believe this?

Your body will tell you. Your energy will shift. Trust that inner guidance.

Wealth Is an Energetic Mirror

Money is a vibration, not a number. It doesn't respond to effort—it responds to energy.

When you start to feel wealthy before the money shows up, the money will come. Because your outer world mirrors your inner frequency.

You don't need to be a millionaire to feel like one. You need to tap into the essence of what you think money will give you: freedom, fun, security, choice, joy. Feel those now. Embody those now.

Play with this idea:

❖ What would I do today if I already had all the money I desired?

❖ How would I feel, walk, breathe, and move if I truly believed money was flowing to me easily?

JOHN PEPPER & ROBERT RUGG

Then do that. Be that. The more you align with that vibration, the less resistance you have—and the faster abundance flows.

Raising Your Vibration Isn't About Perfection

Let's be real—some days you won't feel "high vibe." And that's okay.

Effortless abundance doesn't mean pretending to be positive all the time. It means allowing whatever is present without resistance.

If you're sad, let yourself cry. If you're tired, rest. If you're angry, honor that too. The paradox is, allowing "low" emotions without judgment is exactly what allows them to pass and your natural vibration to rise.

You don't have to raise your frequency. You just have to stop resisting what's lowering it.

Vibrational Practices for Effortless Wealth

Morning Alignment

❖ Start your day with appreciation.

❖ Write down three things you're thankful for and why.

❖ Feel them fully in your body.

Movement

❖ Dance, stretch, or walk in nature.

❖ Let energy move through you.

❖ Joy lives in the body.

Visualization

❖ See yourself already living your dream life.

❖ Feel it in vivid detail.

❖ Smile as you imagine it—it's already done.

Mantras

Repeat aloud:

❖ I am a vibrational match to abundance.

❖ Wealth flows to me easily and effortlessly.

❖ My energy is aligned with infinite receiving.

Celebration

❖ Celebrate even the smallest signs of abundance.

❖ Found a dollar? Celebrate it.

❖ Got a free coffee? Celebrate it.

❖ The more you celebrate, the more you attract.

Real-Life Reflections: Vibrational Wealth in Action

Can you share a specific time when you intentionally raised your vibration—and saw money or opportunities show up almost instantly?

I am intentionally shifting my paradigm to recognize that trading money for goods and services is a severely limiting perspective. The universe is so richly complex, and of all the ways things can come to me, money actually seems like the most boring, not to mention the most simple, short, and straight path.

I was on an Abraham-Hicks cruise that ended in Florida. At some point during the cruise, I met a new friend who I felt a perfectly synchronized resonance with. On the morning of the end of the cruise, we were enjoying breakfast together. I was appreciating the moment and thinking how nice it would be for the conversation to continue. The very next words out of her mouth were that a family member was going to pick her up in an hour—unless I wanted to give her a ride home. My heart jumped for joy.

When we reached her house, the joy continued. I was invited to stay, even though I hadn't booked a hotel. The appreciation just kept expanding. Her cat cuddled with me (a first for them), her daughter gifted me a Starbucks drink, my laundry got done, I drove a Tesla, got a music playlist—all for free. These moments weren't just filled with value—they were overflowing with joy and resonance that money couldn't buy.

What are your go-to practices or routines that help you feel "wealthy" before any money even shows up?

For me, the thought of bringing more wealth into my reality is a flawed premise—my reality is already completely saturated with wealth. It's like a fish asking the universe for more water.

So, my go-to practice is to recognize more and more examples of wealth that are already here. I like to start simple: write down three things I appreciate. Then I expand one of them.

One day it might be my toothbrush. I'll appreciate that I bought it on a road trip, that I used it after a great BBQ meal, and that my dentist says my teeth are perfect. The idea is that any object of appreciation can spark a cascade of joy and wealth recognition. No appreciation is too small. Every moment is already abundant.

Final Thought: Be the Frequency First
When you become the frequency of abundance, wealth can't help but respond.

It's not about trying harder. It's about feeling better.

When you feel wealthy, you naturally think wealthy thoughts, take inspired actions, and magnetize abundant experiences. You move from effort to ease, from chasing to allowing.

So instead of asking, *How do I get more money?* ask:

➤ How can I raise my frequency to match the abundance I desire?

➤ How can I enjoy my life more right now, even before the evidence shows up?

Because when you align with joy, abundance can't help but find you.

64

Chapter 8

The Energy of Money & Receiving – Why Money Is Just a Reflection of Your State of Being

Money Is Energy—Not Effort

LET'S BUST THE MYTH right now: money does not come from working hard.

Money is not earned through sacrifice, struggle, or proving your worth. Money is energy—and it flows based on your state of being.

If you're tense, grasping, fearful, or "needing" money, it tends to disappear or feel just out of reach.

If you're relaxed, aligned, open, and joyful... money shows up unexpectedly. Sometimes through clients, gifts, refunds, job offers, tips, opportunities, or creative downloads.

This isn't just spiritual fluff—it's physics. Your vibration determines what you're a match to. And money, like everything else, responds to energy.

Money isn't a reward. It's a reflection.

How You Feel About Money Determines How It Shows Up

Most people don't have a money problem—they have a receiving problem.

They say they want money, but energetically they're pushing it away with beliefs like:

➤ "I have to work harder."

➤ "I don't deserve it."

➤ "It's wrong to want too much."

➤ "If I charge more, people won't pay."

➤ "Money is the root of all evil."

These thoughts don't align with receiving. They align with lack.

Here's the truth:

❖ Money flows where it's welcomed, not where it's feared or judged.

❖ The more you honor money as loving, neutral energy, the more it can support you.

❖ The more worthy and open you feel, the easier it flows.

How to Become an Open Receiver

Imagine money is like a river. It's always flowing. But if your channel is clogged with doubt, guilt, or fear, the flow slows down or gets redirected.

To receive more, you simply need to unclog the channel.

1. **Examine Your Beliefs About Money**

   Ask yourself:

   ➢ What did I learn about money growing up?

   ➢ What do I believe I have to do to get it?

   ➢ Do I feel safe having money?

   ➢ Do I feel guilty receiving more than others?

   ➢ Bring these beliefs into the light. Question them. Rewrite them.

2. **Shift from Asking to Allowing**

Asking is fine—but don't forget to allow. You've already asked. The universe heard you. Now your job is to align with the version of you who already has it.

This means:

- ➤ Feeling the feelings now.

- ➤ Releasing the need to chase.

- ➤ Trusting it's already on its way.

3. Practice the Feeling of Receiving

Close your eyes. Imagine someone just handed you $10,000 in cash. Or that an unexpected payment hit your account.

- ➤ How does that feel?

- ➤ What do you do next?

- ➤ How does your energy shift?

- ➤ That vibration—that openness—is your portal to more.

Receiving is a Skill You Can Strengthen

Most people are great at giving... but get weird when it comes to receiving.

They deflect compliments, undercharge for their work, or feel guilty saying yes to gifts. But the universe is a two-way flow: giving AND receiving.

If you want more money to flow to you, get good at receiving:

- ❖ Say "thank you" without deflecting.

- ❖ Raise your prices to reflect your worth.

❖ Say yes to support, gifts, ease, and help.

❖ Know that receiving empowers others to give.

Every time you receive with joy, you open the flow.

Money is a Mirror—Not a Master

Money doesn't make you happy. It mirrors back how you feel.

If you believe it will solve all your problems, you'll keep chasing it—and never feel fulfilled. If you treat it as a mirror of your energy, you use it as a tool for alignment.

Instead of asking, "How do I get more money?" ask:

➤ What is my relationship with receiving?

➤ How does money feel in my body? Tight or open?

➤ If money could talk, what would it say about how I treat it?

You may discover that money wants to flow to you—but it needs your invitation.

Your Worth Is Inherent—Not Measured in Dollars

So many people tie their self-worth to money. But you were worthy the moment you were born.

You don't have to earn it. You don't have to prove it. You ARE it. When you know your worth, money starts to reflect that worth back to you.

Say it with me:

"I am worthy of receiving. I don't have to earn it—I allow it."

"I choose to receive with ease."

"I let abundance love me."

Real-Life Alignment: Receiving in Unexpected Ways

Let's get practical. Here are examples of how money might come when you're in alignment:

- ❖ A refund or rebate you weren't expecting.

- ❖ A client messages you out of the blue.

- ❖ Someone gifts you a ticket, coffee, or dinner.

- ❖ You sell something you forgot you had.

- ❖ A payment you were owed suddenly arrives.

None of these require struggle. They require openness.

Ask yourself:

- ➤ Have I allowed for miracles in my budget?

- ➤ Am I open to receiving in ways I don't control?

- ➤ Am I willing to feel wealthy before I see the money?

THE GAME OF INFINITE WEALTH & JOY

Real-Life Reflections: The Cause-and-Effect Flip

When did you first realize that money responds to
energy and not effort?

When you look at life on Earth, it's really obvious that
there is a relationship of cause and effect occurring here.
But cause and effect are so closely and seamlessly linked—
actually composing the two halves of one looping cycle—
that it's possible we've misunderstood the order entirely.
Could it be that effect precedes cause?

I had an epiphany after hearing a lecture titled "Let It
Be Obvious." Suddenly, it hit me—if hard work creates
wealth, how come those working two or three jobs in
physical and emotional exhaustion have the least money?

And yet, those who seem to do the least—like heirs to
a family fortune—receive the most. This flipped my
paradigm. It's not cause then effect. It's vibration first. The
effect—the abundance—is what generates the cause when
you're aligned with it.

As a child, I spent time around wealthy individuals.
Their common trait? A calm, confident attitude grounded
in appreciation and joy. In contrast, during college, I was
surrounded by fear-based thinking: competition,
limitation, and guilt around abundance.

JOHN PEPPER & ROBERT RUGG

Looking back, I now see how belief systems shape our energetic resonance—and our material reality.

Do you have a funny or surprising "money magnet" story?

Yes—one of the funniest money-magnet stories happened when I unconsciously manifested exactly what I feared.

In college, I was surrounded by people who believed it was morally wrong to have "too much" abundance. I absorbed this belief, fixating on "not wanting too much." Over and over, I thought, "I don't want to have too much."

Guess what happened? A relative passed away—and surprisingly left me an inheritance. The universe doesn't hear your negation. It hears your focus. So my focus on "too much abundance" brought exactly that into my reality—effortlessly.

Final Thought: Make Peace with Money and Let It Flow

Money is not your enemy. It's not your boss. It's not your source.

Money is a mirror and a messenger. It reflects your energy and multiplies what's already present inside you.

When you feel whole, loved, and aligned, money simply amplifies that.

When you feel lacking, afraid, or unworthy, money will keep its distance.

So instead of trying harder to get money, become the version of you who naturally receives it.

Open your hands.

Open your heart.

Open your life to more.

The flow is already waiting.

Chapter 9

Letting Go of Struggle & Resistance – Mastering Non-Attachment

The Power of Letting Go

HERE'S A SECRET the mind doesn't want to hear:

Struggle is optional. Resistance is learned.

Most people don't realize that their suffering doesn't come from circumstances—it comes from resisting what is. We fight reality, argue with outcomes, and cling tightly to how we think things should go. And in doing so, we block the natural flow of abundance.

Non-attachment doesn't mean apathy. It means releasing the death grip on how things unfold.

It means this:

- ❖ You care, but you don't cling.

- ❖ You desire, but you don't depend.

❖ You trust, instead of control.

Abundance flows not because of how hard you try, but how easily you allow.

Resistance: The Invisible Repellent to Abundance

Think of resistance as an energetic wall you unknowingly build. It might sound like:

> ➢ "It has to happen this way."

> ➢ "Why isn't it working yet?"

> ➢ "I need this to feel okay."

> ➢ "If it doesn't happen, I'll fail."

> ➢ "I'm trying so hard!"

The more pressure you put on outcomes, the tighter your energy becomes—and the more you slow the flow.

Abundance is like water. It doesn't need to be forced—it flows where there is the least resistance.

Water flows down, not up. Money does too.

Opportunity flows into space, not tension.

What Letting Go Really Means

Letting go is not giving up.

It's the art of releasing attachment to form while remaining in alignment with essence.

You hold the vision—but let go of the timing, method, and outcome.

Here's how you know you've let go:

❖ You feel peaceful, even if it hasn't shown up yet.

❖ You're open to receiving it in surprising ways.

❖ You're not gripping or forcing—it feels like play.

❖ You take inspired action, then return to trust.

Letting go means:

❖ Releasing the need to know.

❖ Releasing the illusion of control.

❖ Releasing the tension around when and how it will come.

Letting Go Creates Space for Miracles

When you let go of your story, your timeline, your expectations, and your fears... you create space. And in that space, magic happens.

The right person calls.

The opportunity appears.

The money lands.

The next step reveals itself.

Because you're not blocking it anymore.

What you resist, persists.

What you release, transforms.

How to Release Resistance and Return to Flow

1. Notice Where You're Holding On Too Tightly

Ask:

➢ Where am I trying to force something to happen?

➢ Where does it feel heavy instead of light?

➢ What am I unwilling to let go of?

Awareness is the first step to release.

2. Practice the "Let It Be Easy" Mantra

Every time you notice tension, say:

"Let it be easy."

This softens your energy and opens the channel of receiving.

3. Stop Arguing with Reality

Whatever is happening, is happening.

Instead of saying "this shouldn't be happening," ask:

➢ How is this actually working for me?

➢ What opportunity is hidden in this detour?

You shift from victimhood to co-creator.

4. Meditate or Breathe into the Present Moment

When you're resisting life, you're almost always in the mind.

Drop into your body. Breathe deeply.

Anchor yourself in now. Because now is where your power lives.

The Non-Attached Manifestor

The most magnetic person in the world is someone who knows what they want—but doesn't need it to feel good.

They're unattached. Light. Open. Present. Grateful.

They're living their life now—not waiting for something to happen.

And guess what?

Things happen faster for them. Because they're not pushing, they're inviting.

Desire plus detachment equals effortless manifestation.

Real-Life Reflections: How Do You Practice Non-Attachment in Daily Life?

If anyone honestly looks back at their life, they will undoubtedly find times where some circumstance they originally thought of as a "bad thing" turned out to be a very good thing. And likewise, circumstances they originally thought of as a good thing turned out to be sharply contrasting.

For example, being late to a work meeting might result in meeting a stranger who offers a better job. And winning the lottery might result in an endless barrage of uncomfortable requests from friends and family for money.

The first obvious conclusion: you do not actually know what circumstances are going to turn out good or bad.

The second obvious conclusion: there is no definitive timeline on which to judge when any occurrence has reached the end of its evolution. Circumstances lead to more circumstances, which lead to more circumstances... forever.

When these two conclusions are fully recognized, it becomes easy to let go. To release expectations. To relax. To be non-attached.

Reality has got you. See it. Know it. Let go of attaching.

Ever Let Go of Something Only to Receive Something Way Better?

I was at a spiritual retreat that had significant importance to me, and part of a group that had access to the front several rows at the venue on a particular day. I got up early, brimming with excitement to be close to the stage.

I got in line early. When the doors opened, the excitement of everyone was palpable.

Seats were filling fast. As I walked in, my eyes spotted an open seat in the third row close to the center. Just as I arrived at the seat, so did somebody else. We both looked at each other. A wave of disappointment emotionally swept over me.

I stopped and turned inward for a moment. As an effortless being, as love, as wholeness, how would I respond?

Good-feeling thoughts arose in the wake of this question:

- ❖ I am at this magnificent event.

- ❖ I am safe.

- ❖ I am healthy.

- ❖ I am surrounded by friends.

- ❖ I have an opportunity to be love.

If this person were my mother, what would I do?

What would I want somebody else to do?

I smiled and motioned my hands downward toward the seat, as if to say, *It's yours.*

As I walked away feeling happiness for the experience this person would have, I noticed a person right in front of me taking a sweater off a seat that was in the very front row, directly centered, and walking away.

I asked, "Are you leaving this seat?"

They smiled and said, "Yup, I'd rather sit back a few rows with my friends than in the front row alone."

The day spent seated in the front row felt like a personal conversation between the speaker and me, with us being mere feet apart.

Try it—let go in love and watch what happens.

What do you have to lose?

Letting Go of the "How" and the "When"
You're not the how. You're not the when.

You're the vibration.

When you stay in the vibe of abundance, joy, peace, and trust—life handles the rest.

Let the universe work its magic. You don't need to micro-manage miracles.

A Personal Story: When I Let Go, It All Came In

There was a time when I desperately wanted to grow my business. I was doing everything "right": Posting, emailing, planning, pushing. And nothing was moving.

One morning, I got fed up. I said:

"You know what, universe? I'm done trying. I'm going to take the day off and do something fun."

I went for a walk. Took myself out for lunch. Listened to music. Watched a comedy special.

That evening, I got three unexpected client messages.

No pitch. No strategy. Just alignment.

The moment I stopped trying to force success... it came to me.

Final Insight: Let Go to Let In

Let go of the need to figure it out.

Let go of the pressure to make it happen.

Let go of the belief that it has to be hard.

And instead:

- ❖ Relax into trust.
- ❖ Open your hands to receive.
- ❖ Let life surprise you.

Because when you stop resisting, life doesn't just get easier—it gets miraculous.

Chapter 10

From Seeking to Being – Living as Already Whole and Fulfilled

The End of the Chase

HAVE YOU EVER FELT like no matter how much you accomplish, something still feels... missing?

That's because the chase never ends. As soon as you get the job, the money, the partner, the house—you want the next thing. The mind is never satisfied. It's built to seek, not to arrive.

But the truth is, what you seek is who you already are.

The wholeness you're searching for out there has always been within you. Fulfillment was never in the thing—it was in the being.

The game shifts completely the moment you realize:

❖   There's nothing to get.

❖   There's only something to realize.

❖   You are already what you're looking for.

How Seeking Keeps What You Want at a Distance

Think about this: when you're seeking something, you are energetically reinforcing the belief that you don't yet have it.

This creates a gap—a vibrational mismatch.

You say "I want abundance," but feel lack.

You say "I want love," but feel lonely.

You say "I want success," but feel not enough.

Seeking is telling the universe, "It's not here yet."

Being is showing the universe, "It's already done."

When you drop the seeking and live from being, you collapse the gap between desire and reality.

You match the vibration of what you want.

That's when it flows to you.

Being Is Effortless. Seeking Is Struggle.

The biggest illusion of the ego is that fulfillment lies just beyond this moment.

But your highest self—the real you—knows:

❖ It's already here.

❖ Right now.

❖ In the breath.

❖ In the stillness.

❖ In the awareness that sees it all.

Being is simple.

It's free.

It's peaceful.

And it doesn't need to prove anything to feel enough.

When you drop into being:

➢ You stop needing things to change.

➢ You stop outsourcing your worth.

➢ You feel complete now... and abundance becomes a byproduct.

Real-Life Reflections: What Helps You Feel Whole and Complete Now, Without Needing More?

Thinking can be paralleled to so many things in physical reality: gasoline, a knife, a car, and electricity.

When these things are used with clear intention and precise focus, they have exceptional power to bring about wonderful outcomes.

However, when these things are used without conscious awareness or focus, there can be wildly disastrous outcomes.

Thought is exactly the same.

The general thought that "I need more"—something more, someone more, somewhere more to be satisfied—is like pouring gallons of gasoline onto unlevel ground and lighting it ablaze, or plugging a cord into a power outlet without knowing where the power cord goes. Roulette at best and a zero-sum game at worst.

Energy follows thought.

Intentionally making a decision to recognize that you have everything you need in this moment—and precisely directing thought toward all the things you already have—generates a completely new feeling, which fosters and encourages completely new thoughts.

You might realize:

❖ I have air to breathe.

❖ I have water to drink.

❖ I have trillions of cells in my body functioning flawlessly.

❖ I have peace of mind.

❖ I have connection to source.

❖   I have unlimited potential within me.

Keep going, slowly, intentionally.

It becomes easier and easier to find thoughts of wholeness and completion right now.

Stepping Into Wholeness Now

Wholeness isn't something you earn. It's something you realize.

Every time you stop striving and just sit with yourself, breathe deeply, and say:

➤   "I am enough now."

➤   "I am already whole."

➤   "I need nothing to be okay."

...you tune into the field of effortless being.

And from there, all things flow.

Here's the paradox:

❖   The less you seek, the more you receive.

❖   The more you allow, the more abundance comes.

❖   The more you relax into wholeness, the more life reflects that wholeness back to you.

Practices to Shift from Seeking to Being

Presence Over Planning

The next time you find yourself future-tripping—pause. Breathe.

Ask: *Can I just be here now?*

Because life only ever happens now.

You'll be shocked how much clarity and abundance flow when you stop running ahead.

Appreciate What Is

Gratitude is the fastest path from lack to abundance.

It says: "I already have so much. I already am so much."

When you feel full now, the universe brings more to match that fullness.

Embody the End Result

Whatever you think your dream life will give you—feel that now.

Want peace? Be still now.

Want freedom? Make one free choice today.

Want joy? Do something playful now.

Don't wait.

Be it. Now.

Sit in Stillness

Start your day with 5 minutes of silence.

Not to "get" anything—but just to be.

Close your eyes.

Feel the breath.

Notice your existence.

Nothing is missing.

That's the whole point.

What Would You Say to Someone Who Still Feels Like They're Endlessly Chasing?

All suffering is thought.

Read that again and sit with it: All suffering is thought.

Life is obvious—so obvious.

Just look openly and objectively at it.

The only thing that ever actually detracts from the perfection of any moment is the thought that something is wrong with it.

Nothing is inherently wrong with this moment or any moment.

It may not be what you think you prefer it to be, but as noted in Chapter 9, you do not actually know what circumstances are going to turn out to be "good or bad," and there is no definitive timeline on which to judge when any occurrence has reached the end of its evolution.

Recognize this. See the obviousness of this.

It's not about bringing this moment into appreciation.

It's about bringing appreciation into this moment.

Chasing things is essentially attempting to manipulate a moment that is already perfect—a paradox.

It is based on a false thought that is the suffering itself.

This path goes nowhere. It's obvious.

Instead, see what is already present in the moment, in every moment, and cultivate an appreciation for it.

A Personal Story: When I Stopped Seeking and Everything Changed

There was a time when I was still chasing success—even in spirituality.

I was doing all the things: journaling, vision boarding, meditating, scripting, working on my "vibration." But it all started to feel like another form of striving.

One day, I sat down and said, "I'm done. I'm not doing another practice. I'm just going to sit here and be."

And in that moment, something shifted. The peace that came over me wasn't something I earned.

It was who I already was.

Under all the effort, the noise, the tools—I found myself.

And from that space:

❖ The right people came.

❖ The money flowed.

❖ The ideas blossomed.

❖ The seeking stopped.

And being... just was.

Final Insight: You Are Already It

You're not becoming abundant—you're remembering you already are.

You're not chasing freedom—you're relaxing into it.

You're not finding yourself—you're releasing what you're not.

So, take a breath. Let the striving go. You are already home.

And from this place of being, all things—love, wealth, joy, creativity—flow to you without resistance.

Not because you chased them.

But because you matched them.

Chapter 11

Expanding Your Reality – How to Open Yourself to Unlimited Possibilities

The Illusion of Limitation

MOST OF US WERE TAUGHT to dream *realistically.*

To be practical.

To play it safe.

We were trained to live inside a small box of what's possible—based on past experiences, societal expectations, or what others told us we could have.

But here's the truth:

Limitations are learned.

Possibility is your birthright.

If you want to live in abundance, you must be willing to question every story that says you can't, shouldn't, or won't.

The only thing standing between you and what you want is your current definition of reality.

The Mind Clings to What It Knows
Your mind's job is to keep you safe.

It does this by sticking to the familiar—even if the familiar is limiting.

So, when a big dream comes through, your mind might say:

- ❖ "That's not realistic."

- ❖ "You don't know how."

- ❖ "It's too late."

- ❖ "Who are you to want that?"

But your infinite self—the being beyond thought—says:

"Of course it's possible."

"That desire is divine."

"Let's go."

To expand your reality, you don't need to force anything.

You just need to stop believing the lies of limitation.

Your Current Reality Is Just a Reflection of Past Beliefs

Everything you're experiencing right now was shaped by your previous vibration—your thoughts, emotions, and self-image.

But the moment you shift your inner state, your outer world begins to catch up.

Your current life is not a sentence—it's a reflection.

And it can change fast when *you* do.

Your reality is flexible.

Your possibilities are infinite.

Your power is **now.**

Expanding Your Awareness to Receive More

You don't attract what you *want*—you attract what you *believe* is possible.

So, if you want to receive more:

➢ You must believe more is available.

➢ You must stretch your imagination.

➢ You must entertain the miraculous.

1. Play in "What If" Land

"What if" is one of the most powerful phrases in the universe.

Start asking:

➢ What if money could come in unexpected ways?

➢ What if I'm more supported than I realize?

➢ What if everything I want is closer than I think?

➢ What if it could be easier than I've been making it?

"What if" opens the door.

"How" slams it shut.

So, ditch the "how" for now. Just play.

2. Normalize the Impossible

The more you expose yourself to people who are living your dreams, the more your subconscious starts to believe it's possible for you.

Follow expanders.

Watch success stories.

Read biographies.

Surround yourself with the energy of "already done."

You'll find your mind shifting from "No way" to "Why not me?"

3. Imagine Wildly and Without Limits

Set a timer.

Close your eyes.

Let your imagination go off the rails.

❖ What would your life look like if there were no rules?

❖ What would you create if money, time, and judgment didn't exist?

❖ Who would you be if you knew you couldn't fail?

Let it be fun. Let it be big. Let it be weird.

Your imagination is not fantasy. It's a preview of coming attractions.

4. Say Yes to the Unfamiliar

When new opportunities show up, the ego might say, "That's too big. Too risky. Too different."

But that's exactly the direction expansion lives in.

Expansion feels like:

❖ Nervous excitement.

❖ Butterflies in your chest.

❖ "Wait, can I really do this?"

❖ "This feels huge, but I can't stop thinking about it."

Say yes anyway.

Expansion Is a State of Being, Not a Goal

Living in expansion means:

- ❖ You're open to more than what you currently see.

- ❖ You trust life to surprise you.

- ❖ You let go of "shoulds" and follow what lights you up.

- ❖ You stop shrinking to fit your past.

Expansion isn't something you reach.

It's something you **embody.**

You're not expanding to get more—

you're expanding because *more is what you are.*

Real-Life Reflections: Dreaming "Too Big" into Reality

When I was a child, I dreamed of being a firefighter.

Cliché? Maybe. But that dream carried a deeper wisdom.

Now I see that what I really admired was the *state of being* firefighters embodied: calm in chaos, clear in decision, inspired in action.

They weren't just brave—they were aligned.

As an adult, I decided to make that dream real.

But the world didn't cheer me on.

Everywhere I looked, I saw reasons why it couldn't happen:

❖ "It's harder to become a firefighter than an astronaut."

❖ "You'll never pass the physical tests."

❖ "If you don't know someone on the inside, forget it."

But I made a quiet decision:

If this role exists in my world, it must be possible for me.

So, I applied. Trained. Showed up.

Even when people laughed. Even when I felt doubt.

❖ I treated every tiny bit of encouragement like gold.

❖ I imagined already being on the job.

❖ I kept showing up—even when it didn't make sense.

And then one day... a letter arrived. A job offer.

It worked.

This wasn't just a career move.

This was *proof.*

Proof that when you believe beyond the limits of your mind, life will rise to meet you.

Real-Life Reflections: Saying Yes to the Unexpected

When I was a kid, I was part of a tight trio. Three best friends, inseparable. The bond was deep—playful, adventurous, pure.

Then one year, I got placed on a different sports team. My two friends started talking about a new kid—someone I didn't know. They laughed about shared jokes. Made plans I wasn't part of.

Jealousy crept in.

Fear whispered, "You're being replaced."

I felt small. Angry. Ready to walk away.

Then came the invitation:

"Want to come hang out with us and meet him?"

My first instinct?

"No thanks." A defensive wall.

But something inside recognized the truth.

My friends weren't leaving me behind.

They were expanding—inviting me into something new.

So, I said yes.

The new kid felt like an instant friend. And soon, our group of three became four.

- ❖ More people meant more games.

- ❖ A new mind brought new ideas.

- ❖ A new house meant new food, toys, and memories.

What started as fear of loss turned into an overflow of friendship.

Saying yes created more than I could have planned.

Focus + Appreciation = Amplification.

Integration Practice: Living Expansion Daily

You don't expand once and stay there forever.

Expansion is a moment-to-moment choice to say yes to life beyond the mind's comfort zone.

Try this:

- ❖ Catch thoughts that shrink you. Ask, "Is this my truth?"

- ❖ Drop into the *feeling* of expansion.

- ❖ Act as if you're already the expanded version of you.

Reflection Prompt:

- ➢ What's one area where you've been believing in limitation?

- ➢ What would happen if you stopped asking *how* and started feeling into *what if*?

> What's one invitation in your life right now that you could say YES to?

Final Insight: You Were Never Meant to Fit Inside a Box

This universe is infinite.

Your being is infinite.

Your potential is infinite.

The only limits that exist are the ones you still believe.

So, ask boldly. Dream big. Let go of logic.

Because the truth is:

You're not here to repeat the past.

You're here to create something brand new.

And the moment you stop asking, **"Is it possible?"**

and start asking, **"How good can it get?"**

...life will show you.

Chapter 12

The Grand Finale – Playing with Life as a Game

Welcome to Level Infinity

YOU MADE It.

Not to the end of anything—but the beginning of something wildly new...

A way of living that's fun, light, abundant, and most importantly—effortless.

This chapter isn't about summing it all up.

It's about reminding you what you already know deep down:

Life was never meant to be a test.

It was always a game.

A joyful, unpredictable, magical game of co-creation.

And you?

You're the one holding the controller.

You're the player *and* the creator.

The game doesn't come with rules.

You make them.

And guess what?

You can change them anytime you want.

The "Secret" to Winning? Stop Trying So Hard

There's a reason things start working when you stop pushing.

When you drop effort, you drop resistance.

And when resistance falls away, life flows in.

It's like trying to fall asleep—have you noticed that *trying* to fall asleep only keeps you awake?

Same with abundance.

Same with clarity.

Same with joy, purpose, love.

You can't force it.

You allow it.

So, what if your new mantra became:

* ❖ "I'll play with this and see what happens."

* ❖ "Let's try this just for the fun of it."

* ❖ "What's the most joyful next move?"

Life loves a playful attitude.

Living from Effortless Abundance Looks Like This

> You follow what lights you up—even if it makes no logical sense.

> You don't force results—you trust the ripple effect.

> You say no to what contracts you and yes to what expands you.

> You feel your way forward, one breath at a time.

> You recognize that every moment is a new opportunity to align.

You're not hustling your way to the top—you're vibing your way home to what you already are.

The Game Gets Easier When You Let Go of the Scoreboard

Some people are always tracking:

✓ How much money is in the bank.

✓ How many likes they got.

✓ How many steps they're ahead or behind someone else.

But this isn't Monopoly.

It's not about accumulating or competing.

It's about alignment.

It's about energy.

It's about joy.

The moment you stop playing to "win" and start playing to *feel good*, **you win automatically.**

- ❖ Joy is the new currency.

- ❖ Ease is the new productivity.

- ❖ Fun is the new strategy.

Play with the Universe Like it's Your Best Friend

Because it is.

The universe wants to surprise you.

It wants to partner with you.

It wants to laugh with you.

It's not judging you.

It's not grading your performance.

It's not holding anything back.

It's simply responding to your vibration.

When you shift from:

"How do I make this happen?" → "I wonder what magic wants to happen today?"

"What should I do?" → "What would feel fun to do right now?"

"Am I doing it right?" → "I trust my path."

...everything shifts.

Life Responds to Your Vibe, Not Your Grind

We've said it a thousand ways in this book, but here it is again—bold and clear:

Effort is optional. Alignment is everything.

You could wake up tomorrow and:

- ✓ Launch a dream project.
- ✓ Meet the love of your life.
- ✓ Get paid unexpectedly.
- ✓ Feel more peace than ever before.

Not because you *worked* for it, but because you **aligned** with it. When you tune into joy, ease, love, and trust—**abundance has no choice but to match you.**

Real-Life Reflections: Playful Joy Turned Into Real Success

I reached a point in my past "traditional life" where I was experiencing "traditional success"—a magnificent job with a great company that paid well, treated me well, and came with a title that made people say "wow."

But the core of that job? Auditing.

Every day was about looking for problems, proving they existed, and telling others to fix them.

Something inside me longed for more play, more fun, more hands-on creativity.

And one quiet morning, a clear inspiration came through: *electrician.*

I saw myself as a child, disassembling electronics and reassembling them into boats and lamps—joyfully immersed in imagination and invention. I remembered the feeling. And the word landed like lightning: **electrician.**

Armed with a Master's degree, a perfect GPA, and 10 years of stellar work experience, I assumed I'd be a shoe-in for an apprenticeship. But the interviews were humbling.

When asked basic questions—like what color wire is used for Neutral—I had no idea. I told them I could learn anything... but they didn't seem convinced.

Still, I trusted. I knew my capacity to learn. I held that knowing lightly, joyfully. Eventually, I got an offer.

And as I progressed through the 4-year apprenticeship, work became more fun, more playful, and more prosperous. I loved learning new skills and applying them in my own artistic way. I loved seeing customers light up. I loved the constant promotions and raises.

The day I passed my Journeyman Electrician Exam, my heart exploded with joy. So did my inbox—with high-paying job offers.

Though I no longer work as an electrician, having a creative, in-demand, high-paying skill is real success in my book.

Joy yields everything, every time.

What Would I Say to Someone Stuck in Grind Mode?
A wise teacher I listen to often says, **"Words don't teach. Only experience teaches."**

So, I'd say this: If you're in grind mode but feel even a slight resonance with Effortless Being or the Law of Attraction... **Give it a go.**

A sincere go.

A genuine go.

An honest go.

You can read and understand all the words in the world, but until you *apply* it, you won't truly know it. Real transformation only comes through one doorway: **firsthand experience.**

Guiding yourself into your own shift is why you're here. It's why *I'm* here. It's why we're *all* here.

There are so many way-showers, teachers, books, and channels. But in the end—**no one is coming to save you but YOU.**

And honestly, you wouldn't want it any other way.

Because, once you prove to yourself that **you are your own solution,** your whole relationship with yourself changes.

You'll see yourself as:

❖ Your own best friend.

❖ Your own superhero.

❖ Your own sovereign, unstoppable, infinite being.

Invincible.

Unlimited.

Indestructible.

Self.

Let This Be the Start of a Whole New Game

As you close this chapter, don't return to "normal life."

Create a new normal. One where:

❖ Receiving is natural.

❖ Rest is productive.

❖ Play is powerful.

❖ Joy is the path, not the reward.

You're not here to struggle. You're here to shine.

To express.

To love.

To feel.

To be—effortlessly.

And to remember that no matter where you go, you are...

The creator.

The channel.

The player of this beautiful, abundant game.

So go ahead—take a deep breath.

Smile.

And ask...

"What would feel fun to create next?"

Because the game is always on.

And you're always ready.

Chapter 13

Robert's Success Story – How Effortless Being Transformed His Life

From Striving to Flow

FOR YEARS, I BELIEVED success came from effort.

I worked hard. I set goals. I chased improvement. I was always reaching for something more. But no matter how many goals I hit, there was still a subtle sense of lack underneath it all—like I was never quite "there" yet.

I devoured self-help books, signed up for seminars, filled notebooks with affirmations, and binged YouTube videos trying to fix myself. I didn't realize it then, but all of it was coming from one hidden assumption:

That something was wrong with me.

That I had to become more in order to feel whole.

Then one day, while listening to *The Greatest Secret* by Rhonda Byrne, I heard these words:

"You are the infinite being having a human experience."

Something stopped.

It wasn't an idea—it was a direct recognition. A remembrance. In that instant, the separate self I thought I had to improve just dissolved. What remained was stillness. Peace. Spaciousness. Joy.

Not the joy of getting something.

The joy of being something.

And not a "someone"—but what I truly am: the open, aware, effortless space in which life appears.

The Shift Into Effortless Being

From that moment on, life no longer felt like something I had to conquer. I stopped striving to become someone. I stopped trying to fix what was never broken.

Instead, I just showed up as I already am—whole, free, complete.

The doing didn't stop—but the struggle did. What used to feel like effort began to feel like play.

I started following what felt expansive, rather than what seemed logical. I let inspiration lead instead of fear. I moved through life without needing to prove anything.

And that's when everything changed.

Abundance Found Me

I didn't "manifest" it by trying harder. I simply aligned with what I already am—and life mirrored that back.

People started reaching out, asking to work with me.

A publisher came to me without effort.

My first book wrote itself in a few days.

Synchronicities multiplied. Opportunities showed up. Coaching sessions unfolded naturally. Money flowed. Joy deepened. I didn't chase abundance—it recognized itself through me.

Because I finally stopped trying to get something—and remembered that I already am everything.

The Joy of Letting Go

Letting go wasn't passive. It was powerful.

Instead of hustling to prove my worth, I allowed it to shine.

Instead of controlling how others saw me, I lived in authenticity.

Instead of obsessing over outcomes, I flowed with presence.

Instead of resisting discomfort, I allowed it to arise and dissolve.

When I gave up the game of fixing myself, the truth revealed itself:

Nothing needed fixing.

Abundance came when I stopped believing I was lacking.

Love came when I stopped chasing it.

Freedom came when I realized I was never trapped.

Key Realization:

I wasn't here to work hard to succeed.

I was here to remember that success flows when I relax into what I truly am.

You don't create abundance.

You allow it.

And when you do, life shows up to meet you—again and again—with more ease, joy, and synchronicity than you ever thought possible.

Your Turn – Let It Be Easy

What if you stopped trying to fix yourself?

What if you paused the search, set down the self-help books, and just rested—right here, right now—as what you already are?

You don't need to become more to receive more.

You don't need to achieve your way into alignment.

You are the abundance you've been looking for.

Let it find you.

Let it flow to you.

Right now, take a breath... and notice:

There's nothing missing.

You are the infinite being having a human experience.

And life responds—not to your effort, but to your being.

Sit with that.

Let it land.

And watch what happens next.

If you want support seeing this more clearly or exploring more resources, visit:

effortlessbeing.net

The next step will reveal itself.

Let it be effortless.

Chapter 14

John's Success Story – Discovering the Game of Infinite Wealth & Joy

"LIFE IS A JOURNEY, not a destination."

There are countless derivations of this quote, most attributed to Ralph Waldo Emerson; pretty much everybody I know would say that they have heard some version of it.

While the quote may be cliché, when I am objective about my life, I find much truth in it. Though, to be perfectly accurate, I would rephrase it to be, "Life is a journey, and an endless series of destinations."

No matter where I am and how many destinations I have reached, I am always eager to set out in a new direction, on a new journey.

It is becoming blatantly obvious at this point:

❖ I am not only a journeyer to endless destinations each day, month, and year, but I literally am the journey itself.

- ❖ I am a lover of change.

- ❖ I am a lover of variety.

- ❖ I am a lover of freedom.

- ❖ I am a lover of the experience of every moment.

When I was younger, I perceived that I was just a physical body within a larger external world. As this vulnerable separate being, I needed to "get" things I lacked from this outer physical world to be complete, safe, and okay.

Therefore, I conceived that the only source of joy was in the outer world. Objects, people, experiences, job titles, salaries, accolades, and appearances were the things I looked to for my sense of self-meaning, self-satisfaction, and self-worth.

And to be honest, there was indeed much happiness and satisfaction to be found in them when I was expressing as my true self. However, my emphasis on trying to get more and more from my external world, multiplied over years, led me to a self-imposed lifestyle that was neither fun nor kind to my mind or body.

My greatest gift came in the form of illness: Lyme Disease.

It was a magnificent physical reflection of both my emotional state of being, and my separate-body perspective of life. In the emotional turmoil of illness, I had a moment which I now recognize as the most significant decision point in my life: live or die.

From the perspective I now hold, happiness and engagement with life literally IS life force. One's excitement to be in this physical world is what keeps them here. If there is no excitement to be here, one will simply no longer be here. There is nothing inherently right or wrong about it; just simple logic. As the creator of our own realities, we will create a new reality if the one we are in is no longer where we want to be.

I decided I wanted to live, that this was my final decision, and that I would change absolutely anything I had to.

The very next day, I came across a video of Dr. Joe Dispenza on YouTube. He made a statement that piqued my curiosity so intensely that I knew it was my path to recovery: "If you are thinking incoherent thoughts all day, you are sending incoherent signals to your body all day."

He then went on to cite all sorts of studies connecting fearful thoughts to measurable physical symptoms. I immediately recognized that I was thinking incoherent and painful thoughts all day, and actually doing so quite consciously; I believed I was supposed to be doing this because everyone around me was doing it!

Dr. Dispenza then made another statement that lit my soul with understanding and excitement: "If your thoughts can make you sick, could they also make you well?" I knew the answer was yes, and I was going to change my health by changing my mind.

Within days of this new understanding permeating my consciousness and practice in guiding my thoughts, I was feeling much better. And, within weeks, I knew I was healed. The blood test results confirming such left my doctors dumfounded.

The healing, though, was the side-effect of my new understanding—my entirely new paradigm that my thoughts had a direct effect on my body. I contemplated this endlessly, and my passion and excitement to understand how this all worked caused my sense of aliveness to surge!

With this surge of aliveness came more and more of a desire to be alive, and more and more of a reflected physical body that would serve as the means to do this. I never looked back... except for now. ☺

For the subsequent several years, excitedly seeking new perspectives on reality became my full-time job. I studied everything "new age" that I could find: quantum physics, the ancient masters of the East, Law of Attraction experts of the West, and everything in between. Ultimately, after digging deeper and deeper (which paradoxically actually meant going broader and broader in perspective), I arrived at the conclusion:

It isn't just mind over matter—mind IS matter.

And who I actually am is neither mind NOR matter.

I literally am my own reality. I am consciousness itself, and the entirety of my external world is actually occurring within myself.

This new paradigm initially caused me to separate more from physical experiences and invalidate the joys of the external world, perceiving that all joy was only within. As the consciousness that was everything, I believed that there was nothing to do but sit in a place and be in my own joy. However, my emphasis on being alone and being the only source of joy for myself ultimately led to a sense of separation—paradoxically, a directly inverse experience from where I began, seeing all joy in the external world.

The yin and yang symbol comes to mind. In one period, I deeply explored the yin. In another period, I deeply explored the yang. Over the most recent period of my life, I have been clearly seeing and choosing to play with a middle, balanced perspective between these two, finding endless joy available within myself, within the external world, and most powerfully within the balanced intersection point of the two. I recognize how the inner joy and the outer joy complement and amplify each other. Through the peace and confidence of an effortless internal being state, I can engage with the external world in a powerfully expressive and deeply appreciative way that attracts truly soul-satisfying physical experiences.

The number of new experiences I have attracted into both my internal and external reality in recent years have been countless. Internally, my sense of self-love, self-confidence, and self-awareness has exponentially expanded, as has my capacity to receive new perspectives, vividly imagine, and focus my mind as I intentionally choose. Externally, I have experienced receiving across the board in new ways and at new levels: finance, friendship, travel, coincidence, gifts, surprises, perspectives, health, encouragement, and mind-blowing moments of exhilaration... jet suit flight anyone?

I have also been clearly seeing how the idea of the journey and the next destination play off one another. Because there is both nowhere to be other than here and now, and somewhere new that I am excited to point myself toward. Both the journey and the destination paradoxically co-exist, and lovingly support and energize the other. Hence, the link between Effortless Being and the Law of Attraction.

I invite you to join Robert and me as we share our greatest understandings at this point on the never-ending journey, in full recognition that we are both inside and outside, nothing and everything, Effortless Being and the Law of Attraction.

Of course... this is all just a story. 😊

———◇◆◇———

Chapter 15

FAQ – Answering the Most Common Questions About Effortless Being & The Law of Attraction

Q: What about action? Don't I still have to *do* something?

Yes—but the *quality* of action matters more than the quantity.

Action from fear feels heavy.

Action from alignment feels light.

When you're aligned, action becomes inspired, easy, and often more effective.

Q: Can anyone really live this way?

Yes. This isn't about special gifts—it's about remembering what's already true for everyone.

You are not broken.

You are not behind.

THE GAME OF INFINITE WEALTH & JOY

You are already it.

Q: What if I have limiting beliefs?

Limiting beliefs only have power when you identify with them.

Start noticing them without fighting them:

➤ "Oh, there's a thought that says money is hard to get."

➤ "There's a belief that says I'm not enough."

But who's noticing the thought? That's your power.

From awareness, beliefs dissolve naturally.

Q: Isn't this just spiritual bypassing?

Not at all.

Effortless Being doesn't ignore emotions—it includes them.

It allows all of life, without judgment:

❖ Fear is allowed.

❖ Anger is allowed.

❖ Sadness is allowed.

And in that allowing, healing happens *without force.*

Q: What if I fall back into effort and fear?

That's okay.

Just notice it. Breathe. Come back to the now.

Presence is always available.

You can return to it instantly—without fixing anything.

Q: Do I need to visualize or say affirmations?

You can—but they're not required.

What matters most is your *state of being.*

If affirmations help you feel abundant, great.

If they feel like effort, drop them.

Joy is the compass. Use what supports it.

Chapter 16

Call to Action – Taking This Into Your Life

This Is Just the Beginning

READING *THE GAME OF INFINITE Wealth & Joy* isn't about learning a new technique.

It's about remembering a way of being that's already natural to you.

Now that you've glimpsed it...

Now that you've felt it...

The invitation is simple:

Live it.

Not as a concept.

Not as a philosophy.

As your everyday experience.

How to Integrate Effortless Being and Infinite Wealth into Your Life

- ❖ Start each day tuning into your infinite nature.

- ❖ Follow what feels expansive and joyful.

- ❖ Trust that life is unfolding perfectly—even when you can't see how.

- ❖ Let go of forcing, controlling, and striving.

- ❖ Say yes to unexpected opportunities and gifts.

- ❖ Practice gratitude—not to get more, but because you already have more than enough.

You're Not Meant to Do This Alone

Integration is easier (and way more fun) when you have a space to reflect, embody, and celebrate your true nature.

That's why we created something special for you:

Join Rob and John for Mirror Zoom Calls designed to help you embody Effortless Being and Infinite Wealth in your everyday life.

These live sessions are a powerful, playful, supportive container where:

- ➢ You're mirrored back to your wholeness.

- ➢ Limiting beliefs dissolve effortlessly.

- ➢ Your natural abundance expands without trying.

Ready to Live This?

To join our Mirror Zoom Program, simply email:

robertrugg123@gmail.com

We'll send you all the details on how to step into this living experience with us.

Because the game is so much easier—and so much more fun—when you have mirrors reminding you:

- You are already infinite.

- You are already abundant.

- You are already free.

Let's play together.

Acknowledgments

WE WANT to EXPRESS our deep gratitude to everyone who walks this journey of remembering their true nature.

To the teachers who pointed us inward.

To the friends who mirrored our light.

To the unseen forces that guided each effortless step.

And to the Infinite Being within all of us—the true source of all abundance, joy, and freedom.

Thank you for playing this game with such courage, laughter, and love.

You are proof that life flows best when it's lived lightly.

Thank You to the Reader

DEAR READER,

Thank you for saying yes to your own expansion.

Thank you for daring to imagine that life can be easy.

That wealth can be natural.

That joy can be the path, not the prize.

In every moment you choose trust over fear, allowing over effort, play over pressure—you change not just your life, but the collective field we all share.

You are a living example of infinite abundance and effortless joy.

We are honored to walk this journey with you.

Keep shining.

Keep playing.

Keep remembering who you truly are.

With infinite love and gratitude,

Rob & John

About the Authors

ROBERT RUGG is the founder of Effortless Being Publications and the creator of the Effortless Being YouTube channel. After a profound realization that he is the infinite being having a human experience, Robert devoted his life to living and teaching from the knowing that abundance, joy, and fulfillment arise naturally when we stop striving and start allowing.

Robert's passion is helping others remember their true nature, embody effortless abundance, and live lightly and joyfully. Through books, coaching, interviews, and retreats, Robert invites others into a new way of being—one rooted in wholeness, play, and infinite wealth.

He believes that when we relax into our natural state, everything we desire flows to us effortlessly—and life becomes the beautiful, joyful game it was always meant to be.

You can connect with Robert by his web site www.effortlessbeing.net or joining the Mirror Zoom Program for live sessions.

———————◇◈◇———————

JOHN PEPPER is a self-described "average guy" with an intense curiosity for the nature of reality and the nature of self. Like many people, this curiosity was born through challenge.

After decades of living a standard life—going to college, getting a job, and following the usual pattern—John perceives that he "gifted himself illness" as a means to spark a completely new paradigm and perspective on life. This new paradigm not only led John to a complete healing, but it opened a new passion, purpose, and understanding that he describes as "absolutely priceless" and "absolutely endless."

For the past several years, John has invested thousands of hours studying the works of countless teachers, traditions, and sciences including Quantum Physics, the Law of Attraction, Dr. Joe Dispenza, Abraham Hicks, Bashar (channeled by Daryl Anka), Neville Goddard, and many others.

For John, *The Game of Infinite Wealth & Joy* is an opportunity to reflect on his own evolution and share his current model of reality and consciousness with the world.

The Game Continues...

The Game of Infinite Wealth & Joy doesn't end with the last page.

It lives in every breath you take.

Every choice you make.

Every moment you remember:

Life is meant to be easy.

Abundance is your natural state.

Joy is who you are.

The next level of the game is already waiting for you—

ready to unfold effortlessly, delightfully, and infinitely.

Keep playing.

Keep trusting.

Keep shining.

The Game of Infinite Wealth & Joy continues... every moment you choose it.

Other Books by Robert Rugg

Available on Amazon and at www.effortlessbeing.net

Awakening to Effortless Being: Realizing Your Infinite Self

A guide to recognizing your true nature beyond thought, effort, and striving—pointing you back to the infinite presence that you already are.

I'm Here, I Feel Good, I Hope You Do Too: Living in Alignment with the Law of Attraction

A lighthearted, practical exploration of how effortless alignment, joy, and presence transform everyday life into a flow of happiness and abundance.

Effortless Abundance: The Art of Thriving Without Struggle

Discover how to shift from scarcity to abundance by aligning with your infinite nature—and allowing wealth, joy, and opportunities to come to you naturally.

THE GAME OF INFINITE WEALTH & JOY

The Mirror Is the Medicine: How Awakening Happens Naturally When You Stop Seeking

An exploration of how reflection, presence, and effortless being open the doorway to healing, awakening, and true transformation.

Infinite Being: The Effortless Journey to Self-Realization

A journey beyond concepts into direct realization of your true self as infinite, effortless, ever-present consciousness.

Stay connected with Robert's latest books, interviews, and programs by visiting:

Effortless Being YouTube Channel or visit his website: www.effortlessbeing.net

Made in United States
Cleveland, OH
23 July 2025

18774418R00080